THE AMERICAN REVOLUTION

AMERICAN HISTORY TOPIC BOOKS

THE AMERICAN REVOLUTION

Richard B. Morris

Illustrations by Leonard Everett Fisher

Lerner Publications Company   Minneapolis

To my grandson,
David,
whose reading about our nation's past
will help shape his role in our nation's future

1985 REVISED EDITION

Revised edition copyright © 1985 by Lerner Publications Company.
Published by arrangement with Lou Reda Productions, Inc.
First published as *The First Book of the American Revolution*.

Library of Congress Cataloging in Publication Data

Morris, Richard Brandon, 1904-
     The American Revolution.

     (American history topic books)
     Rev. ed of: The first book of the American Revolu-
tion. 1956.
     Includes index.
     Summary: Presents the causes and events of the
Revolution.
     1. United States — History — Revolution, 1775-1783 —
Juvenile literature. [1. United States — History —
Revolution, 1775-1783] I. Fisher, Leonard Everett, ill.
II. Morris, Richard Brandon, 1904-   . First Book
of the American Revolution. III. Title. IV. Series.
E208.M874 1985   973.3   85-12878
ISBN 0-8225-1701-9 (lib. bdg.)

Manufactured in the United States of America

     3   4   5   6   7   8   9   10   94   93   92   91   90   89

CONTENTS

The Thirteen Colonies
at the time of the Revolution

CANADA

L. SUPERIOR

MICHIGAN

L. HURON

WISCONSIN
ceded by England
became a state
in 1848

L. MICHIGAN
became a state
in 1837

IOWA
FRENCH until 1803

L. ONTARIO

MAINE
part of the commonwealth
of Massachusetts — became
a state in 1820

NEW HAMPSHIRE

VERMONT
became a state in 1791

L. Champlain

Fort Ticonderoga

Hudson River

Bunker Hill

Bennington

Concord
Boston
MASS.
Lexington

Saratoga

CONN.
R.I.

White Plains

NEW YORK

West Point
New York City

Long Island

L. ERIE

ILLINOIS
ceded by England
became a state
in 1818

INDIANA
became a
state in 1816

OHIO
became a
state in 1803

PENNSYLVANIA

Valley Forge

Philadelphia

Delaware R.

NEW JERSEY

Camden
Princeton
Trenton

MISSOURI
French until 1803

MARYLAND

DEL.

WEST VIRGINIA
part of Virginia
became a state
in 1863

Washington

VIRGINIA

Yorktown

KENTUCKY
became a state in 1792

Guildford Court House

ARKANSAS
French until 1803

TENNESSEE
ceded by spain in 1784
became a state in 1796

NORTH CAROLINA

Wilmington

King's Mountain
Cowpens
Camden

SOUTH CAROLINA

MISSISSIPPI
English until 1779
spanish until 1798
became a state in 1817

ALABAMA
spanish until 1799
became a state in 1819

GEORGIA

charlestown

Savannah

LOUISIANA
French until 1803

FLORIDA
english until 1779
spanish until 1783
French

ATLANTIC OCEAN

N

INTRODUCTION TO REVISED EDITION

On July 4, 1976, New York City's harbor was crowded with tall sailing ships from all over the world. The historic ships were flanked by modern vessels. Many of the ships and their crews had come from distant parts to pay tribute to a people who, exactly two hundred years ago, had proclaimed independence for themselves and liberty for their children and their children's children. The American Revolution was the first great revolution of modern times. The Americans of 1776 had waged a successful war against a great world power and had created a republic that has endured.

The American Revolution is still a part of the lives of all United States' citizens today. They still share the beliefs of the people of 1776 that governments should rest upon the consent of the governed. They believe that the rights of people of every faith and color should be respected. If the United States is to be true to its past, its people must continue to stand up against unfairness, injustice, and ignorance. For those who come to U.S. shores and see the Statue of Liberty for the first time, this nation is still a beacon of freedom.

This book tells the story of the brave people of 1776 who risked so very much to win freedom for what would become the United States of America.

THE ROAD TO INDEPENDENCE

In the early afternoon of July 2, 1776, a tall, painfully thin rider came galloping through the narrow streets of Philadelphia to the Statehouse. In the yard, he reined his horse abruptly and dismounted.

The rider was splashed with mud from head to foot for he had ridden many miles in a summer rainstorm. But he had things more important to worry about than his muddy clothes. He had hurried to Philadelphia to help his country arrive at the biggest decision it had ever made — a decision that would change a large part of the world. Still booted and spurred, he rushed into the Statehouse, where the Second Continental Congress was in session.

The Continental Congress was a group of delegates from all the thirteen colonies then ruled by England, and the rider who had galloped so furiously through the rain to join it was Caesar Rodney, one of the delegates from Delaware.

Like many other colonists, Caesar Rodney was a minuteman — trained to serve as a soldier at a minute's notice. When he received word that he was needed at the Congress, he had been fighting for his rights as an American. He had been leading a group of minutemen against a group of Tories, or Loyalists — colonists who were still loyal to King George III of England. He had rushed straight from the battlefield to Philadelphia.

The Continental Congress was about to vote on the most important resolution ever put before the American people. The resolution had been proposed on June 7th by Richard Henry Lee of Virginia, and it declared that the United Colonies "are, and of right ought to be, free and independent States." Congress had already voted on this resolution on July 1st, but, at that time, the colonies could not reach an agreement. Most of the delegates from Pennsylvania and South Carolina voted against the resolution, and the vote of Delaware was divided.

The next day, the states voted again. This time, South Carolina voted for independence. Two of the Pennsylvania delegates stayed away so that their state's vote would also go for independence. Rodney arrived just in time to swing the Delaware vote in favor of independence. The delegation from New York had no power to vote because that state had not yet made up its mind what it wanted, but later it supported the resolution.

Now all the votes were cast in favor of independence. Two days later, Congress approved the Declaration of Independence that Thomas Jefferson had drawn up with some help from John Adams and Benjamin Franklin. John Hancock, president of the Congress, signed his name on the document in a large bold hand along with Charles Thomson, the secretary.

The break with the mother country was final. There could be no turning back. What had started as resistance to a British army sent to the colonies to force the people to obey certain laws had become a revolution.

HOW DID THE AMERICAN REVOLUTION DIFFER FROM OTHER REVOLUTIONS?

A revolution is a sudden and far-reaching change brought about by force. People may overthrow their ruler, as they did in the American Revolution. There may be a struggle between classes in society. A revolution may start out in a moderate way and end up violently. It may begin by demanding freedom for groups or classes who never had it and end up by using terror and force to enslave everybody.

When the American Patriots declared their independence from England, they started the first great revolution of modern times. Since then, there have been many others. There was the French Revolution, which came only six years after the American Revolution ended. There were successful revolutions in South and Central America and unsuccessful revolutions in Europe. Then, in the middle of the First World War, came the revolution in Russia. Since then, there have been revolutions in Asia and Africa. The American Revolution was the beginning of a time of revolution all over the world.

"All governments derive their just powers from the consent of the governed." When Thomas Jefferson wrote these words in the Declaration of Independence, he expressed the big new idea behind the American Revolution. It was that governments were created to serve the people and had no right to act without the people's consent.

Later revolutions also claimed to speak for the people against their rulers, then gave them harsher rulers to serve. The American Revolution succeeded where others failed. It gave the people a just, democratic government. And one of the reasons why it did this is that it was a different kind of revolution from those that followed.

The American Revolution was not an uprising of the poor against the rich. Both rich and poor fought on the Revolutionary side — large landowners like George Washington in Virginia and the Livingstons and Schuylers in New York, wealthy businessmen like John Hancock of Boston and the Browns of Providence, and countless small shopkeepers, farmers, mechanics, and laborers. Women sewed homespun garments made of colonial materials and stopped dealing with shopkeepers who did not support the American cause. When the men were at war, the women tended the fields and guarded the homes.

On the other hand, many people from these very same classes were against the Revolution. They remained loyal to King George III. Of course, some of these people were royal officials or their relatives and friends who had jobs at stake. Others were rich property owners who would lose their wealth if the revolution succeeded. But a good many were small farmers, particularly in the interior of the colonies—people who did not like being governed by the wealthy colonists who lived along the seaboard and in the bigger towns. These farmers felt that their lot would be better under the King's officials. Then there were tenants who resented the rents their Patriot landlords insisted

on collecting, and the ordinary common people who wanted to keep out of trouble.

The men who led the revolution were sensible and fair. They wanted justice, not revenge. That is why there was no time of terror, why no royal governor was beheaded. In contrast to the French Revolution, the extremists—people who did want revenge—never seized power. No dictator took the place of Congress to rule the people as he thought they should be ruled.

WHAT WERE THE PATRIOTS FIGHTING FOR?

When the Continental Congress declared the thirteen colonies free and independent states, it did not do so without careful consideration beforehand. For almost fifteen months, Patriot troops had been fighting British redcoats. The fighting started on April 19, 1775, but the revolution did not begin until July 2, 1776. The difference is important. In order to understand it, we must go back to the time when the colonies were first settled, back more than a hundred years before the revolution started.

In the beginning, neither the King nor Parliament in England had worked out a plan for governing the colonies. In some colonies like Massachusetts, Rhode Island, and Connecticut, the King allowed the inhabitants to govern themselves and elect their own officials. In others like Maryland, Pennsylvania, and Delaware, the King gave all the land in the colony to a proprietor, or private owner, and allowed him to choose the governor. Still other colonies were governed by the King through officials of his own choosing. These were known as royal colonies. In the course of time, some of the older colonies were turned into royal colonies. This was the case with Massachusetts, where the King took from the colony some of the rights it had had to govern itself and insisted on appointing the governor. In fact, by the time of the Revolution, the King had made most of the colonies into royal colonies.

In order to get the colonies to do what he wanted them to do, the King set up a Board of Trade to watch over them and guide their governors. He insisted that his own King's Council had the right to pass on colonial laws and to hear colonial lawsuits when people were not satisfied with the way they had been treated in the colonial courts.

Parliament also tried to rule the colonies. It passed some laws known as the Navigation Acts. These were intended to regulate trade and to make sure that colonial business did not compete with English business. They were also intended to make sure that any colonial products that England needed would not be shipped to other countries that might pay higher prices.

But no matter how hard the King and Parliament tried to stamp out the spirit of independence in the colonies, it grew and flourished. In all the thirteen colonies, the people made their own laws. Their assemblies voted the taxes and had to approve the salaries paid to the governors, even where these officials had been appointed by the King or the proprietors. Time after time, these assemblies defied their royal governors by refusing to vote them their salaries unless they agreed to the laws the people wanted. When England passed laws to make it difficult and expensive for the colonies to trade with the French and Spanish colonies in the West Indies, the colonists ignored such laws.

Why were the colonies able for so long to ignore the laws and regulations laid down by King and Parliament? The fact is that the British government picked the wrong time to assert its power over them. Slowly the thirteen colonies along the Atlantic seaboard were growing into a nation. By 1776, they numbered 2,500,000 people, almost a third as many as the population of Great Britain. There were many roads for travel by land. The postal service was improving. There were more and more newspapers to keep people even in remote parts of the colonies in touch with what was happening. The English language was changing and becoming more uniquely American. In fact, people were beginning to think of themselves as no longer English. When the Continental Congress first met in Philadelphia, Patrick Henry had said, "The distinctions between Virginians, Pennsylvanians, New Yorkers, and New Englanders are no more. I am not a Virginian, but an American."

Americans were beginning to think of their country as a land of opportunity, as a refuge for the poor and oppressed, as the home of freedom.

At the very time when the colonies were becoming more and more independent in spirit, England was beginning to find her overseas possessions much more difficult to rule. In the first place, they were much larger in area than ever before. England had just won a great victory over France in a world war, known in America as the French and Indian War. That war ended in the year 1763. As a result of the war, England owned huge new areas of land in the New World. They included Canada and all the territory east of the Mississippi River except New Orleans. With the new territory had come new responsibilities, new problems, new expenses.

Wars cost a great deal of money. The war with France had left England with a huge debt. She now hàd to spend still more money to keep troops on her far-flung frontiers, to govern the Indians who lived in her new territory, to set up new colonies. The British people were already taxed very heavily, hence the British government decided that the colonists should pay their share.

The year 1764 saw the beginning of the program to tax the colonies. First, Parliament taxed all sugar brought into the colo-

nies from the French and Spanish West Indies. Then, the next year, Parliament passed a law requiring newspapers, legal documents, and other items to carry a stamp which had to be bought from the government.

There was so much opposition in the colonies to these taxes that Parliament had to repeal the Stamp Act and reduce the duties on sugar. But a new set of acts was passed in 1767 levying taxes on tea, paints, and other articles shipped into the colonies. When the colonists again objected and boycotted—stopped buying British goods—the British backed down once again. In 1770, Parliament repealed all the new taxes except the tax on tea.

Why did the colonists object to paying these taxes? According to the English constitution, the people could not be taxed except by their own representatives in Parliament. The colonists said that it was proper for Parliament to tax the people of England because they elected representatives to the lower house of Parliament, the House of Commons. The colonists insisted, however, that Parliament had no right to tax them since they were not represented. "No taxation without representation!" became the watchword.

THE BOSTON MASSACRE

England planned to use part of the money from the new taxes to pay her colonial officials when the colonists refused to vote them their salaries. This would weaken the power of the colonial assemblies and strengthen the King's power.

In towns and villages, the colonists gathered in angry groups to protest. Feeling ran so strong in Boston that the King sent his scarlet-coated soldiers to keep order there.

Of course, the people of Boston resented the soldiers. They made their lives miserable by shouting after them "Redcoat!" and "Lobster back!"

Then one snowy night in March 1770, some of the English soldiers got into a quarrel with the disrespectful Bostonians. In the excitement, one of the soldiers fired a shot into the crowd. Other shots followed, and five citizens of Boston were killed.

The Boston Massacre, as the colonists called it, aroused fury in the colonies. Nevertheless, the soldiers were given a fair trial in the courts of Massachusetts. They were defended by two Patriot lawyers, John Adams and Josiah Quincy, Jr., who felt it their duty as lawyers to provide the prisoners with a proper defense. Most of the prisoners were acquitted; the two who were found guilty were allowed to go free.

THE *GASPEE*

The Boston Massacre made the Americans determined that there should be no British armies on American soil. Other clashes followed. In June 1772, the British customs schooner *Gaspee* ran aground seven miles below Providence, Rhode Island. Eight boatloads of men from the town attacked it and set it afire. Prominent men planned the attack, but no one was ever punished for it. In the whole town of Providence, the British could not find one person who would identify the guilty men.

20

THE BOSTON TEA PARTY

In 1773, Parliament passed the Tea Act, which gave the British East India Company the right to sell tea directly in America. Because the company could sell its tea cheaper than American merchants who had bought it at higher prices, the colonial merchants were in danger of losing their business.

When the tea company's ship *Dartmouth* reached Boston Harbor, the colonists were ready for it. A company of men dressed as Mohawk Indians rushed to the wharf, boarded the ship, and dumped all the tea into the harbor.

George III was beside himself with rage when he heard the news. He told Lord North, the head of his government, that "the New England colonies are in a state of rebellion. Blows must decide whether they are to be subject to this country or independent."

George III was right. Blows would decide—but not in the way he expected.

THE COLONIES UNITE

The first blow was actually struck by Parliament. In spite of men like Edmund Burke and William Pitt, who were friendly to the colonies, Parliament passed even harsher laws to punish Massachusetts. Americans called them Intolerable Acts. The port of Boston was shut down. The power of royal officials was strengthened, while the powers of the Massachusetts assembly were made still smaller. In addition, a Quartering Act forced the colonists to provide housing for the British troops in America.

Along with these acts Parliament passed another, the Quebec Act, which extended the boundary of Canada southward to the Ohio River. This wiped out the claims some of the colonies had to this territory. It was clear now to everybody that England intended to keep the colonies from growing any bigger or stronger.

The feeling that they must protect their rights by force if necessary began to grow among colonial leaders. In Boston, Samuel Adams organized Committees of Correspondence who wrote letters to other towns and colonies telling them when their rights were in danger. By 1774, there were such committees in almost every colony. They kept in touch with one another and actually did some of the work of government.

Then, in 1774, the First Continental Congress, representing every colony except Georgia, met in Philadelphia. It put into effect a new boycott of British goods and passed resolutions asserting the constitutional rights of the colonists. Just before it disbanded in October, Congress resolved to meet again on May 10, 1775, if by that date England had not changed her policies.

The months between October 1774 and May 1775 were very critical indeed. The government of Lord North in England became more and more hostile to America. The King and his supporters now became the war party. Those who favored the colonies did not have enough votes in Parliament to stop North and the King. Although Lord North proposed a peace plan that offered the colonies a few crumbs, he quickly took steps to punish and weaken the colonies. The New England colonies, along with others, were barred from the vital North Atlantic fisheries upon which so many people had depended for their livelihood. In desperation, Massachusetts began to arm its militia.

THE BATTLE OF LEXINGTON

On the night of April 18, 1775, General Gage sent a company of soldiers to seize some guns and ammunition the colonists had hidden in Concord, a town outside of Boston.

But no sooner were the soldiers on the move than the watchful Patriots of Boston hurried to spread the alarm. Paul Revere, a Boston silversmith, and a companion named William Dawes leaped on their horses to gallop through the dark countryside and warn the Patriots that the British were on the march.

Paul Revere reached Lexington at midnight in time to give the alarm, but he was later captured by the British. A third messenger sped on to Concord.

When the six hundred British soldiers reached Lexington at dawn, they found seventy armed minutemen under Captain Jonas Parker drawn up to meet them. Captain Parker shouted an order to his men.

"Stand your ground!" he ordered. "Don't fire unless fired upon! But if they want a war, let it begin here."

One of the British soldiers fired his musket. An excited British officer shouted, "Fire!"

Eight of the minutemen fell dead, and ten were wounded. The British soldiers went on to Concord to destroy what military supplies they could find.

But on the way back to Boston, they found the countryside swarming with minutemen who attacked them from all sides. Nearly three hundred scarlet-coated soldiers were killed or wounded by the little colonial army that could not even boast uniforms. Only the arrival of fresh troops saved the British from complete disaster.

At Lexington was fired "the shot heard round the world." The engagements of the 19th of April proved that raw militiamen could stand up against trained professional fighters. As the British commander himself admitted, the New Englanders were no "irregular mob."

The British were now on the defensive. Boston was under siege. The War of the Revolution had begun.

THE FIGHT AT CONCORD BRIDGE

THE MEN WHO LED THE REVOLUTION

If you had asked any British official in April 1775 just who the chief American rebels were, he would have singled out two men—Sam Adams and John Hancock.

To look at Sam Adams, one would never have thought that he was a revolutionary plotter. A middle-aged man of middling height and weight, very simply dressed, he looked like a sober and respectable petty official. His father had been a prosperous businessman, but he himself had no luck at making money. On the other hand, he had great talents as a politician and a genius at getting things organized. As one enemy charged, he ate little, drank little, slept little, but thought a great deal and was untiring in pursuing his chief aim—the independence of America.

John Hancock was quite different. He was a wealthy merchant. He dressed in the height of fashion and lived in a handsome mansion on Boston's aristocratic Beacon Hill. He had often disobeyed the British trade laws, and he had considerable trouble with the customs officials. By the eve of the Revolution his business had been hit hard, but he was still the richest man in Massachusetts. When Sam Adams won him over to the Patriot cause, it was a bitter blow to the royal government.

John Adams, of Braintree, Massachusetts, earned the nickname "Old Sink or Swim" because on the eve of the war he had declared that he was determined "to sink or swim, live or die, survive or perish with my country." He had taken a strong stand against Great Britain from the beginning. At the time of the

Stamp Act, he had asserted, "We can never be slaves!"

No Adams would ever be a slave, least of all this short, chunky young lawyer who was Sam Adams's cousin. No other delegate had more influence in persuading the Congress to vote for independence.

The leading patriot from the Middle States was Benjamin Franklin of Pennsylvania, already a world-renowned figure. He had risen from a young printer's apprentice to achieve greatness in half a dozen fields. He became a leading newspaper editor, a great scientist, a brilliant diplomat. He was one of the first to make a practical plan for colonial union. Franklin never forgot the way he had been treated by the British government. Believing that the colonists should know that Britain had been misled by false advice from America, he had helped to publish some letters from royal officials in Massachusetts criticizing the American colonies. For this, England disgraced him publicly and dismissed him from his position as Deputy Postmaster General for America.

Virginia sent to the Congress three men who were as strong and fiery Patriots as those from Massachusetts. First of all there was the lawyer Patrick Henry, the greatest orator of his day in America. Henry had won the spotlight by his famous speech against the Stamp Act, which warned George III that there were limits beyond which even a tyrant dare not go.

The man whom Congress was soon to name to command the American army was another Virginian, well over six feet tall, with a long strong face, blue eyes, and reddish hair. He was shy

VIRGINIA

SIC SEMPER TYRANNIS

WASHINGTON

JEFFERSON

HENRY

and sensitive, and to some people he seemed cold. But he had a quick temper that he tried to keep under close check. Among his friends, he could be both witty and charming. Although he never had much schooling, he was widely read and could write well. As a young man he had been a surveyor, and he was always a fine farmer. He had served as an officer in the French and Indian War, and, although he was one of the biggest landowners in Virginia, he was also one of the leading radicals. He was a great leader of men, truly the central figure of the American Revolution. His name was then on everyone's lips and still is — George Washington.

When Tom Jefferson arrived in Philadelphia from Virginia's Albemarle County, he brought his violin along with him. This did not surprise those who knew the young lawyer well, for he had many talents. He was a very good architect and a clever inventor of all sorts of gadgets. Like so many statesmen of his day, he was interested in many different subjects ranging from law and politics to music and education. He had already written important pamphlets for the Patriot cause. When they picked him to draft the Declaration of Independence, Jefferson's fellow committeemen were sure that they had a man who could put words together and fashion them into a powerful weapon. Their confidence was not misplaced.

These were, perhaps, the chief Patriot leaders, but there were many others. There was Robert Morris of Pennsylvania, a big businessman and financial genius who somehow managed to keep Congress and the army supplied with funds. There was a poor, shabbily dressed newspaperman named Tom Paine who had only just come over from England. His pamphlet *Common Sense,* published in January 1776, did much to arouse the people against George III. There was Charles Carroll of Carrollton, a Marylander and a Catholic, who was concerned about religious freedom for minorities. There was Richard Henry Lee of the famous Lee family of Virginia. Despite his aristocratic background, he never forgot the interests of the common man. And there was the young, spirited Edward Rutledge of South Carolina, who was swung over to the cause of independence by his admiration for John Adams. And, in truth, there were many more. All of them risked their lives for a great idea—the idea of freedom.

HOW DID THE OPPOSING FORCES COMPARE?

The American Revolution could be compared to the fight of David against Goliath. The population of Great Britain was three times that of the colonies. The biggest navy in the world gave her command of the seas. She had bases in Canada and Nova Scotia from which to attack. She had enough money to carry on a war against the colonies and also to hire foreign troops to reinforce her own army. These foreign troops came from Germany, and most of them were known as Hessians.

George III also counted heavily on the fact that almost one third of the colonists were still loyal to him. He knew that sometimes father fought son and brothers fought against each

other. His generals knew that the American armies were untrained and had had little or no experience in battle. They were soon to find out that the American soldiers had to enlist only for a little while. Then many of them went home to their farms and businesses. This helped to weaken an army already short of ammunition, food, clothing, and medical supplies.

The American leaders knew their weaknesses just as well as the British did. But they also knew their strength. First, they were fighting on their own ground while the British were fighting three thousand miles away from home. The colonists were country people who had used guns all their lives, and their rifles could shoot farther and more accurately than the British muskets. Although they had had little military training compared to the British, their experience in fighting the Indians had taught them tricks of wilderness strategy that the British did not know.

Then the colonists knew that they had many friends in England. These people would not support King George in a war against them.

Finally, the Americans had better military leaders than the British. The British generals were too timid when they should have been bold and too reckless when they should have been careful. The Americans had George Washington to lead them, a man who loved freedom and would fight for it even when things looked darkest.

HOW THE WAR WAS FOUGHT

After the Battle of Lexington, the British were in great danger, hemmed inside Boston by colonial troops. If the colonists could drag their cannon to the top of Bunker or Breed's Hill in Charlestown, or if they could capture Dorchester Heights, they could send the British fleet to the bottom of Boston Harbor.

Under Colonel William Prescott the Americans quickly captured Breed's Hill. The British General Howe attacked the hill twice, only to be turned back by murderous fire. At last the colonists' supply of gunpowder gave out, and General Howe won the hill along with nearby Bunker Hill. But the British lost a thousand men—three times as many as the Americans.

Two weeks after the battle of Bunker Hill, George Washington took command of the American troops. He was determined to drive the English into the sea.

Washington was helped by a victory in upper New York State. Benedict Arnold, head of the Connecticut troops, and Ethan Allen, leader of Vermont's "Green Mountain Boys," seized Fort Ticonderoga on Lake Champlain. General Henry Knox, who had left his bookstore to join the army, removed the cannons from the fort and had them hauled to Boston. There General John Thomas raised them into position at Dorchester Heights. With the guns in command of Boston Harbor, Howe had no choice but to get out. Along with a thousand Loyalists, he and his troops sailed to Halifax in Nova Scotia.

35

In only eleven months the colonists had freed New England of British troops.

If the British had been satisfied to blockade the harbors so that no ships could sail in or out, they could have hurt the colonies badly. Business would have suffered, and many people would have been out of work. But instead, the British decided to attack the province of New York, which divided New England from the southern colonies. Then, they believed, they could turn on either New England or the South and crush it bit by bit.

The British first planned to attack New York from the north by way of Canada. But that was just what the Americans thought they would do. Brigadier General Richard Montgomery, an English-trained officer in the American army, hurried north and seized Montreal in November 1775. Then he moved ahead to Quebec to meet Benedict Arnold, who had marched his troops in the dead of winter across the wilderness of Maine. Together Montgomery and Arnold assaulted Quebec, the greatest fortress on the North American continent. But Montgomery was killed, and Arnold was wounded in the leg. The Americans had to abandon the siege of Quebec.

Now the British commander in Canada, General Carleton, thought that the way was clear to strike down Lake Champlain into New York. But at Valcour Bay, in October 1776, Arnold held up Carleton's fleet long enough to upset the British plan.

In the late summer of 1776, the British tried once more to conquer New York, now held by Washington's troops. Sir William Howe, with a huge force of 32,000 men, landed on Long Island. Offshore, to protect him, was a strong fleet of warships under the command of his brother, Lord Richard Howe. Sir William Howe cut the American army in Brooklyn under General Israel Putnam almost to ribbons. General William Alexander bravely fought on to delay the British until what was left of the American army made its escape.

George Washington might have made a desperate stand in Brooklyn, but he would have risked having the rear of his army cut off if the British fleet moved into the East River. Therefore, he moved his troops to Manhattan, avoided a trap on the lower part of the island, and managed to get his main forces out of New York City and up to Westchester. There Howe tried to cut him off. But Washington and his ragged troops fought bravely at White Plains, just long enough to upset Howe's plans. Then they slipped away. For all his 32,000 men, Howe had captured nothing but Fort Washington in northern Manhattan.

Even though their main army had not been captured, the Americans were discouraged. Washington had crossed the Hudson River and was in full retreat before Lord Cornwallis. Things looked very bad.

Howe was sure now that he had nothing more to worry about. He set up a chain of army posts in New Jersey on a line from Staten Island to Princeton and settled into comfortable winter quarters in New York.

But on Christmas night 1776, Washington crossed the ice-choked Delaware River. The night was bitterly cold. Wind, hail, rain, and snow nearly froze the ragged, shoeless American soldiers. When they charged into Trenton the next morning, the Hessian soldiers who held the town were completely surprised. The Americans attacked from opposite ends of the town, and the Hessians were forced to surrender.

Howe was stunned. He ordered Cornwallis to destroy Washington's forces.

Cornwallis thought this would be easy. But Washington completely outsmarted him. In the middle of the night, he stole around Cornwallis's army so quietly that the British officer never suspected what was happening. Early the next morning, Washington attacked the British forces at Princeton.

At the start of the battle, there was great confusion. It looked as though the Americans would surely be beaten back. Then suddenly Washington galloped across the battlefield ahead of his troops, waving his hat to his men. The Americans took courage from this brave act. They drove the British back with heavy losses.

The victories at Trenton and Princeton lifted the drooping spirits of the colonists. Now they had fresh courage for the blows still to come.

A third and last attempt to divide America in half was planned early in 1777 by General John Burgoyne. It seemed to be a perfect plan. Burgoyne was to lead a big army from Canada down Lake Champlain and the Hudson River Valley. A second, smaller force was to move from Lake Ontario eastward through the Mohawk Valley. It would join Burgoyne at the Hudson River. Here both armies would meet a strong force to be sent north from New York City by Howe.

But the men in England who were in charge of the army were not very smart. They approved Burgoyne's plan, but they also allowed Howe to plan an attack on Philadelphia. This left Burgoyne with only two armies instead of three.

At the beginning, everything went according to plan. The main army under Burgoyne took Fort Ticonderoga easily. But as General Philip Schuyler retreated southward with his American troops, they cut down trees to block the roads. The enemy could not follow as fast as they had expected.

Meanwhile, Benedict Arnold brought his troops to the aid of Colonial Peter Gansevoort in the Mohawk Valley. The British were forced to abandon their march eastward toward Albany.

Now Burgoyne's advance was slowed to a crawl. He was running short of supplies. He sent a force of Hessians, Tories, and Indians to capture supplies from the Vermonters at Bennington. But a force of Vermonters and New Hampshire men were waiting for them. The American general, John Stark, ordered his men to attack.

"See there, men!" he shouted. "There they are! We'll beat them before night, or Molly Stark will be a widow."

And beat them they did. Almost everybody in the Hessian force was killed or captured.

In real danger now, Burgoyne pushed southward toward New York, where he hoped to get help from the English forces under Sir Henry Clinton.

But Clinton was a cautious man. He got up the Hudson as far as Kingston, then he decided that his forces were not strong enough to go any further. So he went back to New York for reinforcements.

Meanwhile, Howe had wasted a great deal of time in his campaign around Philadelphia, where he was held up by Washington. It was too late for him to help Burgoyne.

Burgoyne now planned to attack Albany. But the American forces, under General Horatio Gates, met him at Saratoga. There they fought two great battles. In the first, on September 19, 1777, at Freeman's Farm on the west side of the Hudson River, the British suffered very heavy losses. The only reason that the Americans did not crush them was because General Gates refused to send reinforcements to Benedict Arnold.

The second battle of Saratoga decided the fate of the war. It was fought at Bemis Heights on October 7th. Burgoyne was desperate. He was trying to get through and around the Americans in order to reach Albany. But the sharp-shooting riflemen under Colonel Daniel Morgan threw his troops back in disorder.

Then suddenly, out of nowhere, a small man, dressed in a general's uniform and mounted on a huge brown horse, dashed onto the field of battle. It was Benedict Arnold. Shortly before the battle started he had been removed from command by Gates, who was very jealous of him. Now he spurred his horse and galloped straight across the line of fire, leading General Ebenezer Learned's troops to capture the strongest of the enemy points.

Arnold's horse was shot down. He himself was shot in the leg, the same leg that was wounded at Quebec. And Burgoyne,

surrounded by a force three times as big as his own, surrendered.

Saratoga was the greatest American victory so far. It was the turning point of the American Revolution. The English blamed Howe for the terrible defeat of their army. They took away his command and put General Clinton in his place.

But Clinton was an even poorer general than Howe. The King was finally forced to send peace commissioners to America. But since he had not given them power to recognize the independence of the United States, Congress would not have anything to do with them.

The Americans would settle for nothing less than full independence from England.

FRANCE ENTERS THE WAR

Back in 1776 Congress had sent Benjamin Franklin to England's old enemy France to ask for help. Franklin had won the whole French nation to the American cause by his wit, his charm, and his brilliant mind. French officers joined the American army. Among them was the gallant young Marquis de Lafayette. The French government agreed to send money and supplies to America.

But the French king and his ministers did not want to back a losing cause. Once the victory of Saratoga was known, it was clear to them that if they did not get into the war quickly, there was danger that England would make peace with America. In February 1778, France entered the war on America's side.

Other foreigners came over to fight for America. From Prussia came Von Steuben, who became Washington's drillmaster. From Poland came a brilliant army engineer, Thaddeus Kosciusko, who planned the defenses of West Point. And from Poland, too, came the gallant Casimir Pulaski, who was killed leading a cavalry charge in the attack on Savannah.

It was not long before other countries besides France came into the war. They were not so much interested in helping America as they were in taking away some of England's power in the world. Spain joined the side of France. In 1780, a League of Armed Neutrality was organized to protect neutral trade and to keep the English navy from blockading France and Spain. The members of this League were Russia, Denmark, and Sweden. More countries soon joined the League, and England had a world war on her hands.

TROUBLE ON THE HOME FRONT

Now that England had so many enemies, you might think that the Revolutionary War would have ended quickly. But the fact is that it dragged on for almost six years after Saratoga. The main reason was that the central government in America was very weak. Each of the thirteen states refused to yield much power to Congress.

To strengthen the federal government, a constitution was adopted by Congress. This was known as the Articles of Confederation, but it was not until 1781 that all the states agreed to the Articles. By that time, the fighting was nearly over. Even then, the new Confederation did not set up a strong central government. Most power remained with the states. Congress could make no important decision without getting the approval of nine out of the thirteen states. The new Confederation did not provide for a real president with power such as we have today under the Constitution. Congress governed through committees, and that proved to be a very poor way to run a war.

To carry on a long war, a great deal of money is needed. But Congress did not have the power to tax and was always at its wit's end to raise money. France, Spain, and the Netherlands loaned some money to the United States. But Congress had to make up the rest by issuing paper money, the so-called "Continentals."

The states also issued a great deal of paper money of their own. Since neither the federal government nor the states were getting enough income, the paper money was not worth much in gold or silver. By 1780, Americans needed forty paper dollars to buy one gold dollar.

As prices rose and the value of paper money dropped, soldiers began to grumble. In the closing years of the war, they rebelled against their own officers because they had no pay and scarcely enough to eat. Many of them deserted. Some ringleaders had to be shot before the mutiny could be stopped.

Most of the troops remained loyal, however. The army had passed through its darkest days, the bitter winter of 1777-78,

when, half-starved, it went through its agony at Valley Forge, a camp some twenty miles outside of Philadelphia. Washington shared these sufferings with the common soldier, and if their general could take it, so could they.

Despite Washington's popularity with his soldiers, a few officers as well as some politicians wanted to replace him with General Gates. But Washington's own officers came to his support, and he was left in command.

George Washington was truly the outstanding hero of the Age of Revolution. He was a man who always put his country ahead of his own interests. Most of all he wanted two things—victory in the war with England and the building of a strong united nation in the peaceful years to come. No man did more than General Washington to win the war and unite the country.

AN AMERICAN TRAITOR

The greatest shock for the American soldiers lay ahead. Near Tarrytown, on September 23, 1780, three New York soldiers captured a young British officer, Major John André. In his boots they found papers that revealed a plot by Benedict Arnold, then in command of West Point, to turn over that great fort to the British. The fall of West Point would have opened up the entire Hudson Valley to the British. A traitor might have accomplished what all the British generals had failed to do.

Benedict Arnold managed to escape to a British warship in the Hudson. He lived to fight against his countrymen and was well paid for his treachery. André was convicted as a spy and hanged.

THE WAR IN THE WEST

During 1778 and 1779, the area west of the Appalachian Mountains and north of the Ohio River was the scene of some of the bitterest fighting of the whole war. A great frontier leader, George Rogers Clark, led an expedition of Virginia troops against the British and their Indian allies in the Illinois country. Moving across flat prairies, through thickly wooded country, and wading shoulder-deep through icy waters, Clark's men seized most of the old Northwest. Their success was crowned by the capture of the British commander, Lieutenant Colonel Hamilton. Hamilton was known as the "Hair Buyer" because his Indian allies took the scalps of many frontiersmen.

THE WAR AT SEA

On the sea, the little American navy was no match for the huge British fleet. But the Americans captured many British merchant ships and seriously hurt British trade.

There were, too, some daring battles between American naval vessels and British frigates. One of the most famous was the battle between the *Bon Homme Richard* and the British frigate the *Serapis.* The *Bon Homme Richard* was commanded by a Scottish seaman named John Paul Jones who fought for America. John Paul Jones met a fleet of British merchant ships guarded by the *Serapis.* The *Serapis* had forty-four guns, many more than the *Bon Homme Richard.*

John Paul Jones moved in close and ran his ship into the

stern of the *Serapis*. The English captain shouted, "Has your ship struck?"

John Paul Jones replied, "I have not yet begun to fight!"

During the battle that followed, the gun deck of the *Bon Homme Richard* blew up. Flames spread through the ship. But even when his ship seemed about to sink, John Paul Jones and his crew fought on until the British captain hauled down the flag of the *Serapis* with his own hands.

THE WAR IN THE SOUTH

After the British defeat at Saratoga, Clinton had pulled his troops out of Philadelphia and brought them to New York. Now the British planned to capture the South. They thought it would be easy because there were so many Loyalists there.

The British had little trouble seizing and occupying the Southern seaports with their huge navy. They seized Savannah in December 1778 and captured a big American garrison at Charleston in May 1780.

Cornwallis was given the job of winning over the interior country, but he soon discovered that it was not easy. Bands of Americans who were not part of the regular army kept attacking his troops. These men were brilliantly led by Andrew Pickens, Francis Marion, and Thomas Sumter.

The main American army was no match for Cornwallis. At

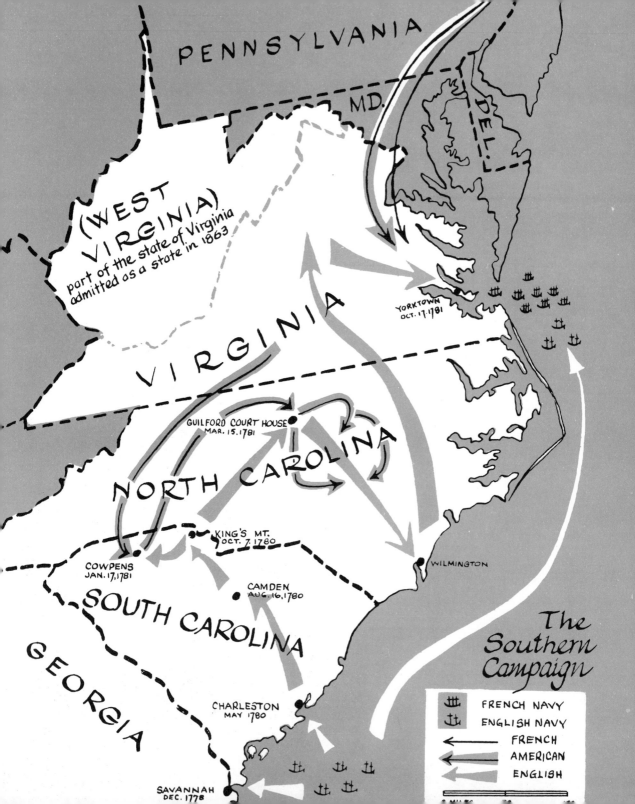

PENNSYLVANIA

MD.

DEL.

(WEST VIRGINIA)
part of the state of Virginia
admitted as a state in 1863

VIRGINIA

YORKTOWN
OCT. 17.1781

GUILFORD COURT HOUSE
MAR. 15.1781

NORTH CAROLINA

KING'S MT.
OCT. 7. 1780

COWPENS
JAN. 17.1781

CAMDEN
AUG. 16.1780

WILMINGTON

SOUTH CAROLINA

GEORGIA

The
Southern
Campaign

CHARLESTON
MAY 1780

⚓ FRENCH NAVY	
⚓ ENGLISH NAVY	
← FRENCH	
← AMERICAN	
← ENGLISH	

SAVANNAH
DEC. 1778

Camden, South Carolina, Cornwallis defeated General Gates. Things looked bleak for the Americans. The British had captured all of South Carolina and were ready to invade North Carolina.

Then slowly the tide turned. At King's Mountain on the border between the Carolinas, the Americans crushed a Loyalist force guarding the left flank of Cornwallis's army.

Some months later, General Nathanael Greene took command of the American army in the South. Greene was a fighting Quaker from Rhode Island, at one time a blacksmith.

Nathanael Greene followed Washington's way of fighting. He never risked a pitched battle with the enemy except on ground he chose himself. Though he rebuilt the southern army, he wisely avoided meeting Cornwallis's main force.

As Cornwallis and his army advanced into North Carolina, Greene sent part of his own army under General Daniel Morgan on a sweep westward. At Cowpens, South Carolina, Morgan's men met a force of British troops commanded by the dashing cavalry officer Colonel Banastre Tarleton. They killed or captured nine tenths of Tarleton's men. Tarleton himself escaped after a saber fight with the American cavalry leader Colonel William Washington, a relative of General Washington.

The armies of Greene and Cornwallis finally met at Guildford Courthouse, North Carolina. The Americans killed or wounded about one third of Cornwallis's troops before they themselves withdrew from the battle.

The English were now tired and dangerously weakened. Cornwallis's supplies were running low. He set off on a two-hundred-mile march to the seacoast. Greene followed in close pursuit. By the time he got to Wilmington, North Carolina, Cornwallis had lost another third of his army.

Still the British general believed he could win. He made spectacular raids deep into Virginia. On one of them his troops almost captured Governor Thomas Jefferson.

At last Cornwallis had to retreat to the coast in order to keep in touch with General Clinton in New York. And when he reached the coast, he discovered that he had stepped into a trap.

This was the moment for which Washington had been waiting six long years. At last he had a navy to cut off Cornwallis's

escape by sea. A French fleet under Count de Grasse was moving up from the West Indies to the Chesapeake Bay area. There was also a good-sized French army in America under Count de Rochambeau ready to help the Americans.

Washington kept his plans a secret even from his own troops. He let the British think that he was going to attack Clinton's forces in New York. In fact, the British general had no idea just where the American and French armies were heading until Washington had crossed the Hudson, struck out southward across New Jersey, and was beyond Philadelphia. Then it was too late to help Cornwallis.

Soon Cornwallis was hemmed in by land and cut off by sea. The French fleet under de Grasse beat off a British fleet which had come to rescue Cornwallis. Together the American and French forces were much stronger than the British.

THE BATTLE OF YORKTOWN

Now the allies laid siege to Yorktown. First, the big guns opened up. The infantry attacked the main defense positions. Then the young and gallant Alexander Hamilton led the attack on the fortifications to the right. He swung himself upon a parapet, brandished his sword, and shouted for his men to follow. Then he leaped down into the ditch, and his men swarmed after him with bayonets fixed. The Americans took the fortifications without firing a shot.

On October 17, 1781, Cornwallis and his army of 8,000 men

laid down their arms.

When the formal surrender took place two days later, the British troops marched out with shouldered arms, colors cased, and drums beating a solemn march. It is said that their band played a tune called "The World Turned Upside Down." This was a song about a mother and her daughter who quarreled. The mother had to get on her knees and beg her daughter's pardon. This was the way England felt when she had to surrender to her wayward daughter, the United States of America. For England it was indeed a world turned upside down.

THE TREATY OF PARIS

Although the fighting was over, the peace treaty, known as the Treaty of Paris, was not signed until 1783. It gave the United States land west to the Mississippi, much of which it had not conquered. It protected America's fishing rights off the Great Banks of Newfoundland and Nova Scotia. But above all, it declared to the world that the United States was a free and independent country.

WHAT DID THE AMERICAN REVOLUTION MEAN THEN?

The American Revolution proved to the world that a nation did not need a king to lead it to victory in war. If the American Republic with a government elected by the people could succeed in the years ahead, then the kings of the world had better start worrying about their crowns.

The American Revolution gave the world a fine example of government by the consent of the governed. This meant that the rulers could act only according to the laws and constitution drawn up by the people or their representatives.

The "unalienable rights" of all people proclaimed in the Declaration of Independence had already been recognized in some state constitutions. Later they were recognized in a Bill of Rights added to the federal Constitution. These rights protected the people from tyranny.

During the Revolution there were changes in the law to make sure that land would not be controlled by a few people. These laws made it possible for free persons to buy or inherit land of their own. The American Revolution helped to make America a country of opportunity for the poor as well as the rich.

The American Revolution was a period of progress and reform. When the Revolution began, the Church of England was the official church in many states. Everybody, no matter what their beliefs, was taxed to support the official church. After the Revolution, church and state were separated, and people were allowed to worship as they pleased.

There were other reforms, too. Prisons were improved, and the laws for punishing criminals were made less harsh. People took more interest in public education and established better schools. In the Northwest, black slavery was forbidden, and steps were taken in the northern states to end it there as well. Even southerners hoped that slavery would come to an end, but that problem was to remain unsettled for several generations.

WHAT DOES THE REVOLUTION
MEAN TO US TODAY?

The American Revolution is as important to our world today as it was to that older world of 1776. Those who live under a free government like that of the United States have much to appreciate. Here we have an elected head of the government who can act only by consent of the governed. Public officials must obey the law just like the rest of us. The American people should continue to guard these freedoms for which the American Revolution was fought.

In school, at games, at home, we can apply the ideals of the American Revolution in our everyday life. We must be willing to let other people talk, even when we dislike what they have to say. We must protect their right to say it. We must guard the civil rights not only of ourselves and our families, but of all groups in our community. We must make sure that everybody in America has freedom of religion, freedom of speech, a fair trial, and equal justice. These are the ideals for which the American Revolution was fought. They are true today as they were in 1776.

FLAGS OF THE REVOLUTION

A variety of flags were carried by Patriot soldiers during the Revolution. There were flags of regiments, flags of states, and a few national flags. The flag shown in the illustration on page 41, with the thirteen stripes of red and white and a circle of thirteen white stars on a field of blue, was officially adopted as the flag of the United States by the Continental Congress on June 14, 1777. Previously the army of Washington used the "Grand Union Flag," which had thirteen red and white stripes, and in the upper left-hand corner the cross of St. George combined with the cross of St. Andrew. In the beginning of the war the naval forces carried a yellow flag with a brownish snake. This was called the "Rattlesnake Flag," and bore the lettering: DON'T TREAD ON ME. The "Pine Tree Flag" of New England shown on page 37 may have been raised over Bunker Hill. Another flag believed to have been borne at that battle was a red standard on which were the words: AN APPEAL TO HEAVEN. At Yorktown the British sent out an officer with a white flag of truce. At the formal ceremony of surrender the redcoats marched out with colors furled.

INDEX

RICHARD B. MORRIS, Gouverneur Morris Professor of History Emeritus at Columbia University, is one of the United States' foremost authorities in the field of American history. He has also taught or lectured at many other universities, including Princeton, the University of Hawaii, and the John F. Kennedy Institute in West Berlin, and is a three-time recipient of a Guggenheim Fellowship. In addition, Dr. Morris is editor of the *Encyclopedia of American History* and the author of numerous books, including the Bancroft Award winner, *The Peacemakers,* and *Witnesses at the Creation: Hamilton, Madison, Jay, and the Constitution.* Presently, he is co-chair of *Project '87,* a nationwide organization devoted to commemorating the 200th anniversary of the U.S. Constitution.

AMERICAN HISTORY TOPIC BOOKS

The American Revolution
The Constitution
The Founding of the Republic
The Indian Wars
The War of 1812